Puppy PALS

German Shepherd PUPPIES

by David and Patricia Armentrout

A Crabtree Seedlings Book

TABLE OF CONTENTS

CRABTREE
Publishing Company
www.crabtreebooks.com

School-to-Home Support for Caregivers and Teachers

This book helps children grow by letting them practice reading. Here are a few guiding questions to help the reader with building his or her comprehension skills. Possible answers appear here in red.

Before Reading:

- What do I think this book is about?
  - *I think this book is about German shepherd puppies.*
  - *I think this book is about being friends with German shepherd puppies.*

- What do I want to learn about this topic?
  - *I want to learn if a German shepherd would be a good pet for me.*
  - *I want to learn how many German shepherd puppies are born in a litter.*

During Reading:

- I wonder why...
  - *I wonder why German shepherd puppies start off with floppy ears.*
  - *I wonder why German shepherds are called working dogs.*

- What have I learned so far?
  - *I have learned that German shepherd puppies make loyal pets.*
  - *I have learned that puppies drink only their mom's milk for the first four weeks.*

After Reading:

- What details did I learn about this topic?
  - *I have learned that German shepherd moms usually have 15 puppies in a litter.*
  - *I have learned that puppies like to chew on toys when teething.*

- Read the book again and look for the vocabulary words.
  - *I see the word **litter** on page 6 and the word **teething** on page 14. The other glossary words are found on pages 22 and 23.*

German Shepherd Puppies

German shepherd puppies are cute balls of **fur**.

Most have two colors in their coat.

Moms have up to 15 pups in a **litter**.

Puppies drink only their mom's milk for the first four weeks.

German shepherd puppy ears start out floppy.

At 20 weeks old,
puppy ears stand up.

Puppies like to chew on toys when **teething**.

When puppies play, they gently bite each other!

German shepherds are a smart **breed**.

Some German shepherds train to become **working dogs.**

Most German shepherd puppies grow up to be **loyal** family dogs.

Glossary

breed (BREED): A breed is a type of animal.

fur (fur): Fur is the soft, thick, hair or coat of an animal.

litter (LIT-ur): A group of puppies or other animals born at the same time to one mother.

loyal (LOI-uhl): Loyal means to be trustworthy.

teething (TEE-thing): Teething means new teeth are coming in.

working dogs (WURK-ing DAWGZ): Working dogs are trained for tasks like search, rescue, herding, and guiding.

Index

About the Authors

David and Patricia Armentrout

David and Patricia spend as much time as possible playing and caring for Gimli, Artie, and Scarlet, three special family dogs.

Websites

https://www.akc.org/dog-breeds/best-dogs-for-kids/
https://www.goodhousekeeping.com/life/pets/g5138/best-family-dogs/

CRABTREE Publishing Company

Written by: David and Patricia Armentrout
Designed by: Jennifer Dydyk
Editor: Kelli Hicks
Proofreader: Crystal Sikkens

Photographs: Cover: photo shutterstock.com/ Jaroslav Francisko, background art shutterstock.com/ Dreamzdesigners. Title Page: istock.com/Bigandt_Photography. Pages 2-3: shutterstock.com/BIGANDT.COM. Pages 4-5: istock.com/Barb. Pages 6-7: shutterstock.com/Jagodka and Lenkadan. Pages 8-9: istock.com/cynoclub and shutterstock.com/slowmotiongli. Pages 10-11: istock.com/Bigandt_Photography. Pages 12-13: shutterstock.com/Rita_Kochmarjova. Pages 14-15: istock.com/cynoclub and shutterstock.com/Ssilverartist. Pages 16-17: shutterstock.com/Victoria Antonova. Pages 18-19: shutterstock.com/DTeibe Photography and ANURAKE SINGTO-ON. Pages 20-21: shutterstock.com/Stone36 and Versta. Page 22 top photo: shutterstock.com/Sergey Kamshylin.

Library and Archives Canada Cataloguing in Publication

Title: German shepherd puppies / by David and Patricia Armentrout.
Names: Armentrout, David, 1962- author. | Armentrout, Patricia, 1960- author.
Description: Series statement: Puppy pals | "A Crabtree seedlings book". | Includes index.
Identifiers: Canadiana (print) 20210190906 | Canadiana (ebook) 20210190914 |
ISBN 9781427157645 (hardcover) |
ISBN 9781427157652 (softcover) |
ISBN 9781427157669 (HTML) |
ISBN 9781427157676 (EPUB) |
ISBN 9781427157683 (read-along ebook)
Subjects: LCSH: German shepherd dog—Juvenile literature. |
LCSH: Puppies—Juvenile literature.
Classification: LCC SF429.G37 A76 2022 | DDC j636.737/6—dc23

Library of Congress Cataloging-in-Publication Data

Names: Armentrout, David, 1962- author. | Armentrout, Patricia, 1960- author.
Title: German shepherd puppies / David Armentrout, Patricia Armentrout.
Description: New York : Crabtree Publishing, 2022. |
Series: Puppy pals - a Crabtree seedlings book | Includes index.
Identifiers: LCCN 2021017197 (print) | LCCN 2021017198 (ebook) |
ISBN 9781427157645 (hardcover) | ISBN 9781427157652 (paperback) |
ISBN 9781427157669 (ebook) | ISBN 9781427157676 (epub) |
ISBN 9781427157683
Subjects: LCSH: German shepherd dog--Juvenile literature. |
Puppies--Juvenile literature.
Classification: LCC SF429.G37 A68 2022 (print) | LCC SF429.G37 (ebook) |
DDC 636.737/6--dc23
LC record available at https://lccn.loc.gov/2021017197
LC ebook record available at https://lccn.loc.gov/2021017198

Crabtree Publishing Company

www.crabtreebooks.com 1-800-387-7650

Printed in the U.S.A./062021/CG20210401

Published in the United States
Crabtree Publishing
347 Fifth Avenue, Suite 1402-145
New York, NY, 10016

Published in Canada
Crabtree Publishing
616 Welland Ave.
St. Catharines, Ontario L2M 5V6